Finding Your Way Back:

The Credit Recovery Road Map

Paul Alan Storm

Finding Your Way Back: The Credit Recovery Road Map.
© 2009 Paul Alan Storm
ISBN 978-0-578-01876-8

Published by Lulu

TABLE OF CONTENTS

To my past and present clients.

You continue to inspire me.

Chapter 1

Been There...Done That!

What keeps you awake at night? I'm not asking about your noisy neighbors or the beagle barking across the street. When you lay there in the silence, what *really* keeps you tossing and turning?
Is it...

- Where you and your family will live after the foreclosure?

- How out of control your finances feel?

- Whether you'll ever be able to pay all these bills?

- Whether or not you can come back from this bankruptcy?

- Whether you'll ever be able to get this behind you?

Odds are, you're reading this book because you are one of the millions who is "there." By "there," I mean the big bad wolves of bankruptcy, foreclosure, consumer credit counseling, and/or a buffet of other credit problems are huffing and puffing at your door.

For some of you, the house has already been blown down. Others of you are holding on to the last straw of your lives. Then there are those of you who spot the wolves approaching on the horizon, and you don't know what to do. Just thinking about their arrival is causing your health and relationships to suffer.

My friend, I have a message for you: No matter how fierce the wind is blowing against you at this moment, I assure you the big bad wolves of bankruptcy, foreclosure, and credit problems will not win.

In the end, **you** will win.
You **will** find your way out.
You **will** find your way back.

I know.
I've been there.
I've done that.

Once upon a time, I owned investment properties. I rented to tenants who didn't just pay late. They eventually chose to not pay at all. Plus they destroyed the properties. I was left with real estate I couldn't rent or sell without investing tens of thousands of dollars I no longer had.

As the financial dominoes fell, I was pinned by bankruptcy and foreclosure. What I vowed would never happen to me, did. I was humiliated. I was angry with myself. I wondered if I could ever get this "monkey" off my back. I feared this was fatal. In time, however, and after much hard work, I ditched that "monkey" and found my way back. Through the process I learned painful but valuable lessons.

Then in the fall of 2003, I literally stumbled into helping others suffering through bankruptcy and foreclosure get back on their feet.

As word spread that I knew how to help consumers find their way back after bankruptcy and foreclosure, ten clients turned into a hundred and a hundred turned into a thousand and a thousand turned into thousands. **While helping them, I became a credit recovery expert because I dealt with *every* possible credit situation.**

So when I say I know the way back, I *really and truly* know the way back. I haven't just read books and watched a CBS special report. Courtesy of the "school of hard knocks", I know the way back.

I know the way back from pretty much any credit problem.

I even know the way back from bankruptcy and foreclosure.

I know the way to beat those wolves.

I know the trail by heart.

I know how to get you to where you want to be *without* being taken advantage of just because you have less than perfect credit.

I know what credit dead-ends to avoid so you don't waste your valuable time or money.

I know how to help you take back control of your credit.

I know the way back.

If you will let me be your guide, you, too, will find your way back.

So let's get started. The sooner we start, the sooner you too can look back and say, **"Been there…done that!"**

Chapter 2

Five Stones

I need to let you in on a little secret. Well…perhaps "secret" is not the right word. Maybe a better phrase to describe it is "a little known fact." I was *in* the finance industry, but it wasn't until I personally experienced credit problems that I realized how invisible yet essential this "secret" was in helping me find my way back.

Whatever you prefer to call it, this relatively unknown detail is vital to finding your way back. That's why I'm telling you upfront. Ready or not here it is:

You are NOT alone.

Before you conclude I'm a few cards short of a full deck thinking that "you are not alone" is a "secret", please allow me to explain.

I am not referring to the supernatural, extraterrestrial, or human connection. I am speaking of federal and state acts and agencies which guard consumers 24/7.

At times on this journey to find your way back, you may feel completely alone. But it isn't just you against the night. It isn't just you against the world. It isn't just you against the creditors. The federal and state governments stand with you in your corner and are watching out for your consumer rights.

I affectionately refer to these governmental acts and agencies as the "five stones." When you face the goliaths standing in your path to recovery, you need to know these five stones are in your back pocket:

1. <u>Fair Credit Reporting Act</u> (FCRA) To avoid having you fall asleep on me, I won't publish the entire 86 pages. Instead here's a breakdown of what the Fair Credit Reporting Act means to you:
   - ➢ You have the right to know what is in your credit file including your credit scores.
   - ➢ You have the right to know if information in your credit file is being used against you.
   - ➢ You have the right to dispute errors, and credit reporting agencies must correct or remove those errors within 30 days.

> You have the right to approve who has access to your credit report including your employer.

> You have the right to sue anyone who violates the FCRA.

As you find your way back, I guarantee you will need to exercise at least one of these rights provided by the Fair Credit Reporting Act.

2. The <u>Equal Credit Opportunity Act</u> (ECOA) prohibits credit discrimination based on age, marital status, national origin, race, receipt of public assistance, religion, and sex. When a creditor turns down your request for credit, they are legally bound to tell you why. If you have been declined for credit based on these factors alone, it is a violation of federal and state law.

3. The <u>Fair Debt Collection Practices Act</u> (FDCPA) bans debt collectors from abusing, deceiving, and unfairly collecting debts from you. They can only call you between the hours of 8 a.m. and 9 p.m. unless you give them permission. They cannot use intimidation, and if you request in writing for them to stop contacting you by phone, they must! Speaking of writing, within five days of calling you,

they must send a letter notifying you who it is you owe, how much, and how to resolve the debt or dispute it. The next time a debt collector calls you remind them of all of the above!

4. The <u>state attorney general's office</u> where you live exists to defend and protect all your rights including your consumer rights. Creditors and debt collectors *will* violate your rights. When they do, refuse to be a victim and contact your state attorney general's office! **www.findingyourwayback.com** and Appendix D have every state attorney general's contact information.

5. Last, but far from the least, is the <u>Federal Trade Commission.</u> (FTC) The Federal Trade Commission carries the biggest stick in the land when it comes to credit and creditors. If you are getting jerked around by a creditor or the credit bureaus, the Federal Trade Commission (877) FTC-HELP is where you turn. When you inform a creditor or debt collector you're going to call the FTC, in most cases they will react like I did as a child when my older sister said, "I'm going to tell Dad!!" Like me not wanting my Dad involved, your creditors and debt collectors do not

want any trouble with the FTC because they know who will win!

I don't know the details of your situation. I don't know every twist and turn in the road ahead for you as you find your way back. What I do know is that on every step you take, these five stones are in *your* back pocket, and you are not alone.

Chapter 3

What to Pack
To Find Your Way Back

Breaking news! You're going on a trip! Whether or not you're an experienced traveler means little, because this trip is like no other you have ever taken. The destination is not Orlando or Cancun.

The destination is finding your way back.

Take it from someone who has made this journey many times; the key to finding your way back is in what you pack. Let me forewarn you; some of the items you will need are not fun or pleasant. This trip you are embarking on is **not** for rest and relaxation. At times, your journey will be as harsh as an arctic winter, but if you follow my packing checklist, you'll be prepared for the trail ahead. Based on my experience here's what to pack to find your way back:

1. **Power.** You will need three powers:

   A. The power of **a positive attitude**. Time and time again you hear, "Attitude is everything," and it rings true even in finding your way back. It's easy to keep a positive attitude when life is puppies and roses, but when the wolves of bankruptcy, foreclosure, and credit crisis scratch and claw at your soul that's when you find out what you're really made of. Whether it's through the assistance of your faith, circle of friends, or reading books like this one, you will need to pack the power of a positive attitude to find your way back.

   B. The second power you'll need to take is **staying power**. Finding your way back is like running the Boston Marathon. It requires endurance and perseverance despite cramping, dehydration, and sheer exhaustion. There will be mountains and obstacles which may seem as big as Mt. Everest that I will guide and cheer you through, but ultimately you must choose to stay and run the course. Having personally run the race and assisted thousands of others, I guarantee you will be tempted to quit more than once. I know those who did wave the white flag. Some threw in the towel a mile into the journey, while others quit on the last hill. But for the many who broke the tape and found their way back, I will forever carry their celebration in my heart. To sit with them and watch tears of joy stream down as they sign for their new home is unforgettable. When I ask why they didn't quit, the most frequent answer is: I kept my eyes on the prize…the finish line.

C. The final power to pack is **the power of knowledge**. Knowledge is power. Want to know how I became an expert in this field? When I went through my personal bankruptcy and foreclosure, I was *in* the lending industry, but lawyers and lenders were not telling me what I needed to know. So I spent evenings and weekends surfing the internet, visiting my local library and bookstores, reading everything related to credit, bankruptcy, and foreclosure.

My challenge to you is: become an expert yourself. Reading this book is just the beginning. Attend seminars and workshops. Visit websites like **www.findingyourwayback.com**. Between the internet, the local library, college libraries, and bookstores, read everything you can about bankruptcy, foreclosure, consumer credit counseling, and other credit issues.

As you research and learn, be sure to follow the rule of the two "R's": **R**eputable and **R**ecent. Check to make sure the books and articles are written by reputable people who are educated and in the trenches of the finance industry. Too many so called "experts" have little or no actual experience working in the finance industry!

Also, make sure the information is recent; and by recent I mean written in the last 6-12 months. The credit industry alone has undergone a major transformation in the 6 months prior to the writing of this book, so it's important to stay current. The more you know, the more you are empowering yourself to find your way back.

Okay, so you've packed the power to find your way back. Now it's on to the 2nd item you need to put in your backpack:

2. **People.** Brace yourself because this is one of those unpleasant pieces I mentioned earlier. The first part is easy. Besides the normal friends and family, trustworthy people such as certified credit counselors, attorneys, realtors, and loan officers will play a vital role in your recovery. If you haven't yet, begin cultivating relationships with reliable

individuals in these professions because you *will* need them in the present and future.

The other group of people you should pack to find your way back is far from easy or fun, but they *can* help. I'm referring to anyone with whom you had or have a joint credit account which *even* includes former boyfriends, girlfriends, husbands, or wives. When I ask clients what caused their credit problems, one of the most popular answers involves a relationship that ended. In the break up or the divorce, one party usually gets the short end of the stick. They either get stuck with all the debt, or their credit rating is destroyed when the other person does not pay the joint account on time. For the good of both parties' credit, declare a "ceasefire" and work together to pay off and close the joint account(s). Later in the book, I'll be going into more detail about this whole issue, but for now accept the fact that these people from your past *can* contribute to your present credit recovery.

3. **Paper.** To find your way back you'll also need to pack essential paperwork such as bankruptcy papers, divorce decrees, foreclosure and deed in lieu of foreclosure notices, short sale agreements, and any other type of credit related document. Begin

thinking about where these documents may be because you *will* need them later.

4. **The final item you'll need to gather to find your way back is CPS. CPS** is a term I invented which stands for Credit Positioning System. You're probably familiar with technology called GPS (global positioning system) which is now in cell phones, certain brands of automobiles, and navigational devices. GPS allows you to accurately locate where you are and navigates you to where you want to be.

   Like a GPS, the **CPS** you need to pack allows you to find your credit location and navigate to your credit destination. It is critical to know where you are now in relationship to great credit, poor credit, bankruptcy, foreclosure, consumer credit counseling, etc. You need to know how far "back" is. You need to determine where is "here" and "there."
   In the next several chapters, we'll be using **CPS** to determine the extent of finding your way back.

Chapter 4

What's Your 10-20?

Imagine someone calls you for directions to your home. What's the first piece of information you need to know in order to give the best directions? Seems to me their physical location is essential. You can't give directions from "there" to "here" when you don't know where "there" is. The same is true in finding your way back. The journey begins with identifying where you are when it comes to your credit.

Back in the old cb radio days when users wanted to know the location of someone they would ask, "What's your 10-20?" The other party would respond with something like, "I'm at the corner of Vine and Maple, heading east." To find your way back credit-wise, you first have to identify what your credit 10-20 is. Knowing where your credit location is involves the **CPS** (credit positioning system), which I mentioned in the last chapter. The **CPS** I've devised helps you identify your credit location through credit maps and signs. Just as street, shopping, and road signs determine where you are physically, so too, there are credit signs which indicate where you are in relation to finding your way back.

Let's begin with the **CPS** credit signs you need to look for:

CPS CREDIT SIGNS

Credit Scores

Nothing will give you a better and faster snapshot of where your credit location is than your credit scores. Look at your credit scores just as you would a highway mile marker sign. They are your credit location, not your credit destination. You are on a journey to find your way back. Your credit scores identify whether you are at mile marker 51 or 351, so it is essential you know what they are.

Because the whole credit scoring system is continually being changed and improved, what I'm about to say will probably be dated by the time this book is published. There are numerous credit scoring systems which you can find more information on at **www.findingyourwayback.com**, but here I just want to focus on the most commonly used system.

Currently, the standard credit scoring system involves three credit scores issued by the three recognized credit bureaus; Equifax, Experian, and TransUnion. Each of them depends on a credit scoring system called "FICO". "FICO" stands for FAIR ISAAC COMPANY, which is the company that created the credit scoring formula. At the time this book is being written, the credit scoring formula goes something like this:

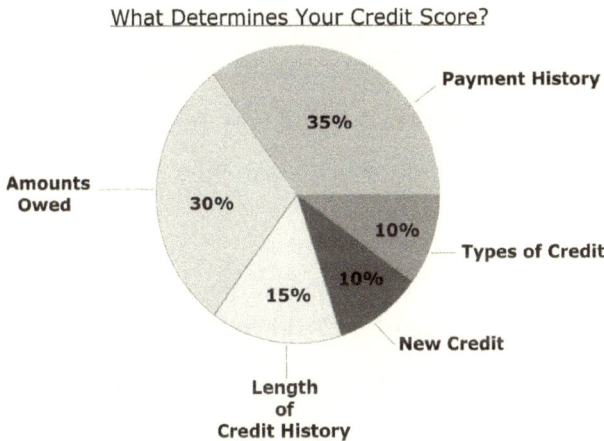

What Determines Your Credit Score?

Payment History
35%

Amounts
Owed
30%

10%
Types of Credit

10%

15%

New Credit

Length
of
Credit History

In later chapters, this pie chart will be discussed in depth, but for now, here are some quick observations:

1. To have credit scores, you need to use credit. Paying cash for everything is excellent, but to have a credit score, you need to use 2-3 lines of any type of credit for at least several months. Those 2-3 lines of credit can be as small as $200 limit secured credit cards or a personal line of credit from your bank. To build credit scores, you can

either pay off your balance each month, or pay your monthly payment. Either way, you will develop a credit score.

2.   The recipe for establishing good credit scores requires the ingredients of paying your credit on time, keeping balances low (50% or less of your credit limit), and establishing a long, solid credit history. It's not rocket science, as some make it out to be. With the FICO credit scoring system, credit scores range from 300-850. Generally speaking, the higher your credit scores are, the shorter your journey is to finding your way back, and the lower your scores are, the longer your journey is to finding your way back.

Currently, lenders consider 740+ to be great credit. Anything less means you need to improve your credit scores. Perhaps you're wondering, like other consumers, **"How long does it take to raise credit scores?"** If you follow the recipe of paying your bills on time, paying down your balances, and lengthening your good credit history, your credit scores *will* begin to rise after 30 days.

I can't tell you exactly how many points your credit scores will rise after 30 days. I've seen some consumers improve 10 points and others 100 points. Many different factors are involved, and I will weave those factors in throughout the rest of this book. For now, though, the great news is whatever your credit scores are, you **can** find your way back, and I will show you how!!

ASSIGNMENT

Here's your assignment right now: If you do not know what your current credit scores are, get on the internet and carefully type in **www.annualcreditreport.com** or call (877) 322-8228 and discover your credit scores. This is the central website established by the three credit bureaus and recommended by the federal government where you can obtain a copy of your credit report.

Please keep in mind when you see your credit scores that they are just a sign in the credit positioning system (**CPS**) which reveals your credit location, not your destination. So go pull and print your credit report now; then, come back to learn two more **CPS** credit signs to identify your credit 10-20.

Public Records

So now you know the first **CPS** Credit Sign: your credit scores. But as I previously said, credit scores identify your credit location, *generally speaking.* Your credit report

---

also contains vital information called "Public Records" that can override what your scores are. For example, you may have credit scores of 659, 701, and 681, but if you have a bankruptcy within the last 7 years showing on your "Public Records", certain creditors will not approve you no matter how high your credit scores may be.

Creditors extend credit based on a variety of factors, and public records such as bankruptcies, foreclosures, deed in lieu of foreclosure, short sales, judgments, and tax liens can cause you to be turned down for a loan or credit card. If you have public records showing on your credit report, I highly recommend finding your original paperwork from your bankruptcy, foreclosure, deed in lieu of foreclosure, short sale, judgment, and tax liens, and verifying that the information is being accurately reported. Later, I'll discuss in depth what to do if your credit report contains wrong information. For now, though, keep your paperwork close for later reference because it will be a vital part of finding your way back. If for some reason you cannot find your paperwork, it is important you obtain a copy and keep it for your records.

- For bankruptcy paperwork, contact your attorney, trustee or the U.S. Bankruptcy Court in your area.
- For foreclosure, contact your local Register/Recorder of Deeds.

- For deed in lieu of foreclosure and short sales, contact the lender involved.
- For judgments, contact your local district court.
- For federal tax liens, check with your local IRS office or call (800)829-1040.
- For state and local tax liens, contact your treasury departments.

Paper or Plastic?

While your credit scores and public records identify your current credit location, the next **CPS** sign, "Paper or Plastic", indicates where your future credit position will likely be. It is a sign of things to come, because "paper or plastic" shows your credit direction.

Take a few minutes to pull out and review the last 6 months of bank and credit card statements. What do you see?

Which balances are ballooning?
Which balances are shrinking?
Are you losing ground in one or both of them?
Is your cash shrinking while your credit card balances are ballooning?

What are your credit card balances compared to their limits?

I have worked with thousands of consumers who filed bankruptcy. Take a wild guess at what the number one reason for bankruptcy is. If your answer had something to do with credit cards, you win the prize! If plastic is becoming your primary means of supporting your lifestyle, a credit storm is brewing on your horizon. The choices you make today with "Paper or Plastic" will determine where your credit "10-20" will be tomorrow. The longer you wait, the longer your journey to find your way back will be.

EXERCISE

Okay. So **Credit Scores**, **Public Records**, and **Paper or Plastic** are the three key signs to identify your credit "10-20." Let's now connect the dots of these three signs of the Credit Positioning System and plug them in to a map of the big credit picture. Pretend with me there is a country called "Creditland." Creditland looks like this...

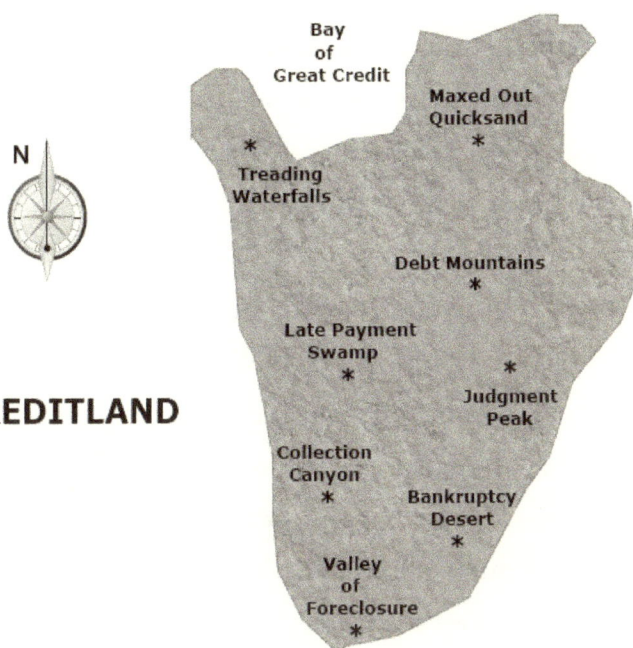

CREDITLAND

Bay
of
Great Credit

Maxed Out
Quicksand
*

*
Treading
Waterfalls

Debt Mountains
*

Late Payment
Swamp
*

Judgment
Peak
*

Collection
Canyon
*

Bankruptcy
Desert
*

Valley
of
Foreclosure
*

N

Touching Creditland's northern coast is the **Bay of Great Credit**. It's what Zihuatanejo, Mexico was to Andy Dufresne in *The Shawshank Redemption*.

It's our dream.

It's our destination.

It's the end of the journey of finding your way back.

It's where our credit scores sail 740 and above, and our plastic takes a vacation.

It's where public records have been carried out to sea by the tide.

There is only the peaceful sound of waves breaking on the beach and palm trees blowing in the wind.

Because you're reading this book, though, chances are good you're **not** floating in the **Bay of Great Credit**. Perhaps you're stuck in the **Maxed Out Quicksand** or lost in **Debt Mountains**. Maybe heat exhaustion has you wondering if you'll ever make it out of **Bankruptcy Desert**.

Whatever your situation may be, here's what I want you to do. Grab the credit report you pulled and your most recent credit card statements. Spread them out on your desk or kitchen table and compare them with the map of Creditland. Circle the location or locations that identify your credit 10-20… your credit location. If both bankruptcy and foreclosure are part of your present and past, circle them. Circle everything that describes your credit situation. These are the wolves huffing and puffing threatening to blow your world apart. Now, I want you to mark your place here and flip to page 112 of this book, because I have a message for you. It's a message I encourage you to put on your refrigerator, mirror, desk, or some other place where you will regularly see it. It's a message I hope you read out loud and memorize:

"This is my *location*, <u>not</u> my *destination*."

My friend, where you circled on the map of Creditland is not the end of the road for you. At this moment, you may struggle to believe those words. You may think you're too far south…too far gone…to ever find your way back, but this is just your location not your destination. Take it from someone who has been there personally and professionally and has helped thousands who have been there…you ***will*** find your way back.

Yes, you will. It's time, right here and right now, to turn this around. It's time to map out the way back to the **Bay of Great Credit**. It's time to blaze trails across the **Valley of Foreclosure** and stomp through **Late Payment Swamp**.

Your dreams are waiting.

Time Out

Before we move on to the meat and potatoes of finding your way back, I'm calling a time out.

Take a deep breath. Grab a drink and kick back. Gather your thoughts, look around your credit location now, and engrave this moment in your memory. **Never** forget you were here. **Never** forget what it feels like to be in this pickle. You will need these memories when finding your way back gets tough and you're tempted to quit and return to this place. Take your time. Whenever you're ready, turn the page. It's time to leave for good. It's time to find your way back.

Chapter 5

"This Way!"

Grand Canyon National Park reports that around 400 hikers a year typically have to be rescued in the Grand Canyon due to medical emergency or getting lost. With the extreme landscape and conditions there, it's easy to see why.

When it comes to the credit maze of finding your way back, it's also relatively easy to lose your way. So many voices are coming at you. One says, "Don't use any credit." Another financial expert counsels, "Use credit to build your credit scores!" Before you know it, you're running around in circles like a dog chasing his tail getting nowhere.

What's the solution? I would suggest the answer is the same advice the Grand Canyon National Park gives to avoid ending up needing search and rescue: Begin with a hike led by an experienced hiking guide. To find your way back, you need to follow someone who knows the way out of **Collection Canyon**. You need a guide who won't get lost in **Late Payment Swamp**. You need a seasoned guide who, even in the blinding sand storms of **Bankruptcy Desert,** shouts, "This way!"

After helping thousands of consumers just like you find their way back, I am qualified to be your guide. Even though I may not know every detail of your story, I still can help you. Wherever your location may be in the imaginary country of Creditland, I know the way back. I know it like the back of my hand so let's get started.

Because we are all at different credit locations, no way back is the same. You may be starting your way back from the **Debt Mountains** while your neighbor is scaling **Judgment Peak**. To be able to help everyone, I've consolidated the way back into four different trails as seen in the map:

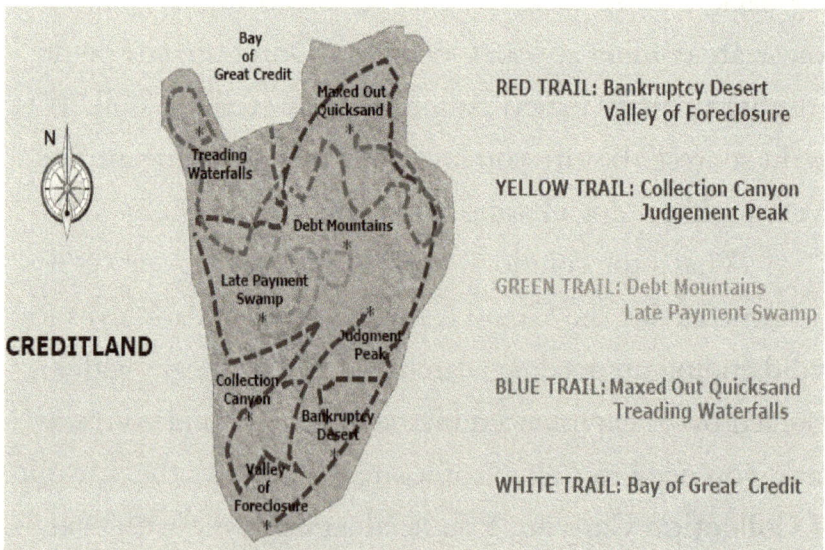

RED TRAIL: Bankruptcy Desert
Valley of Foreclosure

YELLOW TRAIL: Collection Canyon
Judgement Peak

GREEN TRAIL: Debt Mountains
Late Payment Swamp

BLUE TRAIL: Maxed Out Quicksand
Treading Waterfalls

WHITE TRAIL: Bay of Great Credit

If your credit 10-20 is bankruptcy or foreclosure, take the Red Trail.

If collections or judgments consume you, hike the Yellow Trail.

Follow the Green Trail if **Debt Mountains** or **Late Payment Swamp** surrounds you.

Or if you find yourself maxed out and treading water, stick to the Blue Trail.

      In the following chapters, I will be describing in detail the above trail maps so you can find your way back. You are more than welcome to skip to the chapter which deals with your current credit situation. My suggestion, however, is to read all the chapters, regardless of your credit location. Right now you may be in **Collection Canyon** or **Judgment Peak**, so you want to hike the Yellow Trail first, but what happens if those collections and/or judgments become too much and you file bankruptcy? In that case, then knowing the Red Trail becomes very important! Or, let's say you want to stick to the Blue Trail to find your way back from **Maxed-Out Quicksand** and **Treading Waterfalls**. To get the big picture, it wouldn't hurt to read about the Green, Yellow, or Red Trails.

      Whatever you choose to do, keep in mind the goal is to reach the White Trail, which leads to the **Bay of Great**

Credit, which means you found your way back. To me, as your guide, that's all that matters!

So…lace up your hiking boots, grab your water bottle, cover yourself with sunscreen and insect repellant, and follow me. The way back is… this way!

Chapter 6

The Blue Trail:
Maxed Out Quicksand
& Treading Waterfalls

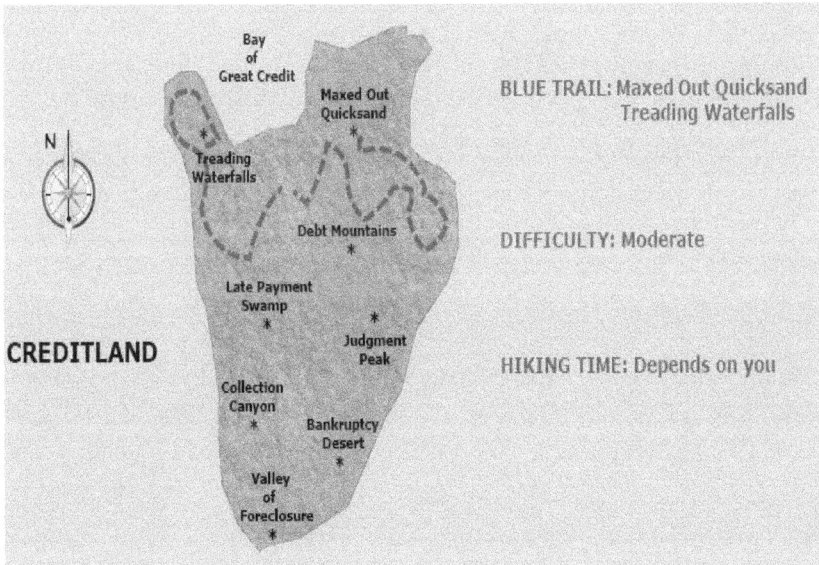

Bay
of
Great Credit

Maxed Out
Quicksand

N

Treading
Waterfalls

Debt Mountains

Late Payment
Swamp

CREDITLAND

Judgment
Peak

Collection
Canyon

Bankruptcy
Desert

Valley
of
Foreclosure

BLUE TRAIL: Maxed Out Quicksand
Treading Waterfalls

DIFFICULTY: Moderate

HIKING TIME: Depends on you

Christmas…car repairs…Emergency Room visit…reduction in work hours…divorce…one shopping spree…that's all it takes in life to relocate you from sunning yourself on the **Bay of Great Credit** to wading through the dangerous **Maxed-Out Quicksand** and **Treading Waterfalls** of the <u>Blue Trail</u>. One minute you're floating; the next you're sinking, and sinking fast.

Sometimes the <u>Blue Trail</u> is our own doing, due to poor planning or being a shopaholic. Other times, circumstances far beyond our control put us on the <u>Blue Trail</u>. I'm not here to point fingers; I'm here to help you find your way back to the **Bay of Great Credit**.

Now some of you may be thinking, "Sure, I've got a lot of debt, and my credit cards are close to maxed out. I'm living paycheck to paycheck. I'm not getting ahead or falling behind, but I'm not paying anything late or letting bills go to collection. I'm okay. I still have great credit." Maybe you do….then again, maybe you don't.

Remember this pie chart from earlier?

What Determines Your Credit Score?

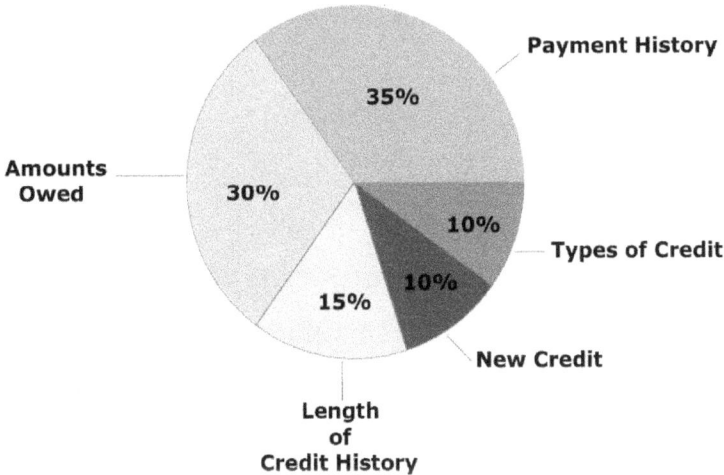

Payment History 35%

Amounts Owed 30%

10% Types of Credit

10% New Credit

15% Length of Credit History

30%. That's how much your credit balances influence your credit scores. The FICO (Fair Isaac Company) credit scoring system, which is the standard in the lending industry, deducts points from your credit score when you have balances which are higher than 50% of your credit limit.

For example, if you have a credit card limit of $300, and your balance is $275, that high balance will lower your credit scores, even if you're making your payments on time. I've personally seen such a scenario lower a client's credit scores by 53 points, and his scores dropped so significantly he was not able to qualify for a mortgage to buy his new home. Even on a small credit card, how much you owe can cost you big time on your credit scores; but not all is lost. If you are on the Blue Trail, you can quickly recover and find your way back to the **Bay of Great Credit** by completing the following mission:

<u>Your Mission:</u>

1. **<u>Track your credit scores</u>**. Some credit card companies make this a breeze by posting your credit scores each month when you access your account online. If your credit card companies don't, go to **www.annualcreditreport.com** or call (877) 322-8228 as recommended earlier in the book to see if your credit scores are at least 740. The credit meltdown over the last few years has caused the credit industry to raise the bar of what great credit is. A score of 660 used to be considered a good enough score to qualify for about any type of mortgage. Now, 740+ is considered to be the **Bay of Great Credit!**

2. **<u>Pay down your balances</u>**. As you can easily see from the pie chart, how much you owe plays just as important a role in high credit scores as paying on time. For maximum credit score benefit, carry balances that are no more than 30% of your credit limit.

   Glance at your credit card statements and grab a calculator. Divide your balances by your credit limits.

What percentage of your credit limits are your balances? If they exceed 30%, <u>pay down your balances</u>. To do so may involve finding extra money. Here are some simple suggestions for coming up with extra cash:

A. Review your budget and cut out the fat. Start keeping a record of your spending habits by buying a ledger or using one of the great computer programs or internet websites available for tracking expenses. Begin the habit of entering your income and every expense to see what *percentage* of your income is going where. You may be surprised how much going out for lunch every day is costing you over the course of a month. Examine what you're spending your hard earned money on and change your ways so you can put more money towards paying down your balances.

B. Sell the tuba. What I mean is sell items you don't need or use to raise extra cash. Just yesterday I received a call from a past client whose employer has cut his and everyone else's wages in an attempt to help the company survive the tough economy. He sold his hunting equipment and riding lawn mower to pay bills. Craigslist.com is just one example of a free website where you can advertise your boat, mountain bike, or baseball card collection which is just sitting there collecting dust. Turn them into cash to pay your debts.

C. Find a part-time job or business to increase cash flow. In the past, I delivered pizzas and sold my blood plasma to make extra money. Laugh if you want to, but it helped pay the bills. Toss your pride and do whatever it takes to bring in extra income.

3. **Contact your creditors to see if raising your credit limits is possible**. This is a short term solution to maintain or improve your credit scores, but it is a dangerous one, so keep focused on the goal here: Find your way back on the Blue Trail to the **Bay of Great Credit**. You're not raising your credit limits, so you can go out and use more plastic.

Blue Trail People, there is your mission, and I can guarantee you one thing; if you don't complete your mission, before you know it, you will end up on the Green Trail. And as you'll find out in the next chapter, you *don't* want to be on the Green Trail.

Chapter 7

Green Trail:
Debt Mountains
& Late Payment Swamp

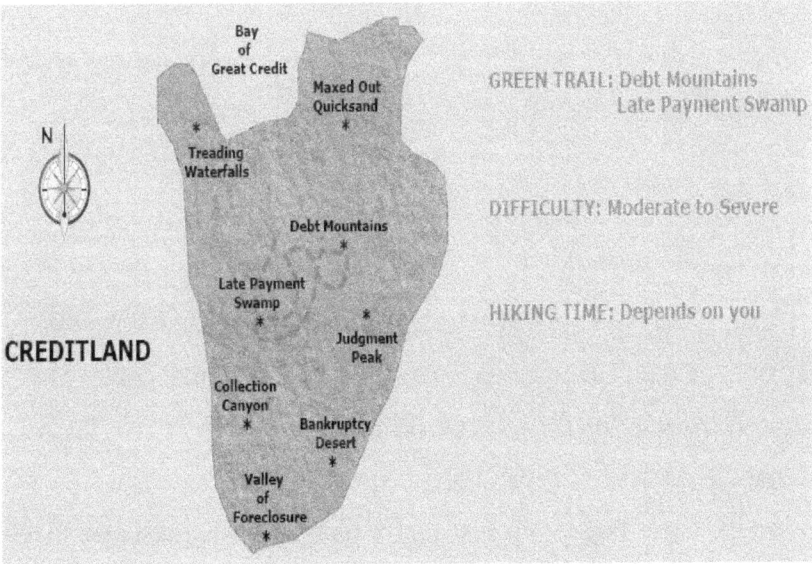

Bay
of
Great Credit

Maxed Out
Quicksand
*

GREEN TRAIL: Debt Mountains
Late Payment Swamp

N

Treading
Waterfalls

Debt Mountains
*

DIFFICULTY: Moderate to Severe

Late Payment
Swamp
*

HIKING TIME: Depends on you

Judgment
Peak

CREDITLAND

Collection
Canyon
*

Bankruptcy
Desert
*

Valley
of
Foreclosure
*

When I was a child, I lived in the West Indies. Just about once a week, my parents would take us to the beach. I remember one particular afternoon watching a group of boys playing in the ocean with a soccer ball. The tide was going out, so anytime the ball got loose, it quickly floated into much deeper water, and one of the boys would swim after it. The boys' parents kept warning them to be careful and move closer to the shore, but the boys shouted back, "Don't worry. We're fine!"

Shortly thereafter, the peacefulness of a fun day at the beach was permanently shattered by those same boys' and parents' screams. A boy who had swum out to get the ball couldn't fight the swift tide, and he was being carried out into the Caribbean Sea. All anyone could do was watch in horror as he disappeared. They never even found his body.

I think it's human nature to ignore or downplay warnings. Even with finances and credit, the tendency is to assume, "I'm fine. I know what I'm doing. That'll never happen to me." Before you know it, you're drowning in debt, standing on the <u>Green Trail</u> looking up at the **Debt Mountains** and wading through the **Late Payment Swamp**. One late payment leads to two, two leads to three, and suddenly three has turned into a notice of foreclosure proceedings. Your credit scores nose-dive, and **The Bay of Great Credit** becomes a distant memory.

There's an old sailors proverb that reads:

Red sky at night...sailors delight.

Red sky in morning...sailors take warning.

From personal and professional experience, I can tell you the <u>Green Trail</u> is that "red sky in the morning", warning you about an impending financial storm on the horizon. It's coming, and it's coming for you.

Perhaps the very thing you said would never happen is about to make a direct hit on your life. That is, unless you get serious, turn around right here and now, and find your way back using the <u>Green Trail</u>.

There are 6 primary steps to finding your way back on the <u>Green Trail</u>. The first four are covered in this chapter. The final two steps will be covered in the next chapter, for reasons you will soon see.

Step #1: <u>Know the payment terms of your credit cards and loans.</u> Verify whose name(s) are on the account(s) and who is an authorized user. Read the fine print to determine what is considered a "late payment" and will be reported to the credit bureaus as such. The key is what your "billing cycle" is. For some creditors, any payment after the due date listed on your statement is considered late. Most creditors, however, offer a 15 or 30 day grace period and will report you as "late" if you pay on day 16 or 31.

What to Do When an Ex is Hurting Your Credit

Here under payment terms is as good a spot as any to discuss the difficult subject of an ex ruining your credit by not paying a joint account they agreed to pay. **The painful truth is your creditors do not care what your divorce decree says regarding who is responsible for what debts.** All that matters to them is the fine print on *their* contract which states that if you are on the account, you are responsible to pay on the account. So if you have a joint account with an ex who is slow paying or letting the debt(s) go into collection or foreclosure, here are your options:

A. Communicate with the creditor(s) by phone and letters stating what the situation is.

B. Ask the creditor(s) what your options are. Can the account be closed or frozen so no further debt can occur? Can your ex be removed as an authorized user?

C. If the joint account is a secured loan such as a mortgage or car loan, consider taking your ex to court to force them to refinance in their name alone or sell so the joint account is closed.

D. If it is financially possible for you, take over the payments so no further damage is done to your credit. **If need be, ask the creditor(s) to reach a settlement with you so you don't repay the full amount.**

E. Consider bankruptcy if your credit has already been destroyed by your ex and you have little or no financial resources to pay off the debt. Bankruptcy will be discussed in detail later in this book.

When it comes to an ex hurting your credit, there are no easy answers or solutions. There is no magic wand or instant fix. In most cases, it is a long painful process controlled by the payment terms you previously agreed to with your creditors. When you know those terms, then it's time to move to step#2 on the <u>Green Trail</u>:

Step #2: <u>Verify the accuracy of creditor's reports about you</u>. I can't tell you how many clients I've worked with who had creditors reporting late payments when there weren't any! That's why it is so important to pay by personal check or online; so you have proof of when the payment was made. When you do pay online, make sure you print and keep the receipt for your records. Those of you who are paying by cash, cashier's check, or money order, I would strongly advise you to open your own checking account for the sake of payment proof. Cash receipts and copies of cashier's checks and money orders are easier to lose, and it's more difficult to prove when the payment was actually made.

How to Dispute Errors on Your Credit Report

If you discover errors on your credit report, **www.findingyourwayback.com** gives you an overview of the process and lists many other websites related to this subject. For now though, here's an overview of what to do when creditors report wrong information on your credit report:

1. Know your rights outlined in the Fair Credit Reporting Act (FCRA) and Fair Debt Collection Practices Act (FDCPA). If the error involves a lawsuit or judgment, check with your state attorney general's office to verify what the "statute of limitations" are in your area. Creditors are limited to a period of time in which they can come after you.

2. Go to **www.annualcreditreport.com** because it allows you to electronically dispute errors which means the issue should be resolved faster. On each

of your credit accounts, you have an option to check a dispute button then upload or fax in dispute letters (see **www.findingyourwayback.com** for sample letters) and the proof such as cancelled checks, receipts, bankruptcy papers, etc. Typically 30 days later the issue is resolved, and the credit bureaus mail the updated results.

3. If issues arise such as an uncooperative collection agency, you can file a consumer complaint using the direction of **www.ftccomplaintassistant.gov**. In case you haven't guessed it yet, the Federal Trade Commission **www.ftc.gov** is the law of the land, and every creditor has to answer to them.

4. You may be tempted to hire what is called a "credit repair" company which promises to *fix* your credit fast for a significant fee. Save your money. **There is no such thing as *fast* credit repair and <u>you</u> can do it yourself.** Stick to clearing up your credit by going through the proper channels of www.annualcreditreport.com, the credit bureaus, and the Federal Trade Commission.

Once you've verified what is true…

Step #3: <u>Consult a qualified credit counselor</u> who is a member of the National Foundation for

Credit Counseling (**www.nfcc.org** (800)-388-2227) or Association of Independent Consumer Credit Counseling Agencies (**www.aiccca.org** (866)-703-8787).

CAUTION:

I feel the need to pause for a moment and clarify that I'm not talking about the companies filling the airways with promises of only paying back a fraction of what you owe while they charge you enough for their services that you might as well have paid your original creditor the full amount. **I have worked with many clients who previously sought the help of a "debt counselor/negotiator" that ruined their credit even more! The "debt counselor" either did not pay the creditor on time, or they did not pay them at all. These clients were eventually forced to file bankruptcy.** Besides these issues, there is also the risk of tax liability on any amount of forgiven credit card debt so check with your tax accountant as well.

The credit counselor I am speaking of is a trained and reputable non profit agency that will genuinely look out for *your* well being. Besides cost, the main questions you need to ask are:

- Will you help me do a budget to avoid future problems?
- Will you sell my information?

Lay everything on the table with them so they see the full landscape of your **Debt Mountains** and **Late Payment Swamp**. Then, allow them to use their experience and expertise to create a specific action plan for you to find your way back to and stay in the **Bay of Great Credit**.

Step #4: <u>Return to the old fashioned way</u>. This is the way back detailed for the <u>Blue Trail</u> in the previous chapter. You pay down your debt by adhering to a strict budget, selling items to raise cash, and taking a second job. I realize this is much easier said than done, because once you start falling behind it's like a snowball rolling down the hill. It becomes almost impossible to catch up or stop due to the double whammy of amount due to make the account current and late fees. Because of this, I want to jog off on a rabbit trail to discuss a very critical issue in finding your way back. That critical issue is foreclosure, or rather, avoiding foreclosure.

AVOIDING FORECLOSURE

Here on the <u>Green Trail</u> and Step #4, foreclosure can pop up as quickly as a thunderstorm in rainy season when you're in the **Debt Mountains** or **Late Payment Swamp**.

In 2008, 1 in every 54 homes was in some form of foreclosure. Homeowners are taking a huge beating in this difficult economy, and I am running into consumers who are seriously considering just walking away from their homes. In case you didn't know, **foreclosure is considered worse than bankruptcy by the lending industry, so no matter what your long term plan is you should do everything possible in the short term to avoid foreclosure!!** Here are suggestions (some obvious) if you fall far enough behind on your mortgage or property taxes that your lender or local taxing authority begins foreclosure proceedings:

1. Learn what the foreclosure laws are in your state. You can contact your local Recorder/Register of Deeds or the Sheriff's Department, who in most

states holds the foreclosure auction, and they will be able to give you correct information regarding the time you have left to do something with your property.

2. Prioritize your bills. When you are scraping to get by and having to pick and choose which bills to pay, put the mortgage at the top of the list and wait to pay the medical bill(s).

3. Consider renting out a room, rooms, or the basement for extra income. I realize it's awkward to have someone else living in your home, but if it keeps you from foreclosure, go for it.

4. Borrow money. Perhaps you have the money in a 401K, or you are fortunate enough to have family or friends who can lend you the money to stop foreclosure. **Carefully consider this option only after weighing all the factors involved including your home's present market value and what you owe.** If you are in a city or neighborhood where values are plummeting, do not waste your savings or retirement money if the return on your investment is negative. You are better off letting the home go into foreclosure.

5. Sell the property. Sorry to be so obvious. The difficulty in today's real estate market is selling a home for at least what you owe. The epidemic of foreclosures in some neighborhoods has significantly dropped home values. So you may have to negotiate with your mortgage company to do what is called a "short sale." A "short sale" is when the two of you agree on a sales price to sell your home for less than what is owed. They will report it as a "short sale" on your credit report, but it is still far better than a foreclosure.

   If you do sell your home by "short sale", make sure you contact your tax accountant. The 2007 Mortgage Forgiveness Debt Relief Act changed tax laws so sellers who do short sales on their primary residence do not have to declare the shortage as income as long as it is less than $2 million. For example, if your short sale ends up being $20,000 less than what you actually owe your mortgage company, you may not have to pay income tax on the $20,000. To be safe ask your accountant how it applies to your specific situation and short sale.

6. Pursue "forbearance" with your lender. Perhaps you are behind on your mortgage due to a temporary reduction in income, and you fully

expect to get back on your feet. Your lender can reduce or suspend your mortgage payments for a period of time, and/or they can arrange to take the amount you are behind and put it on the end of your mortgage when you pay off the loan.

7. Attempt a "loan modification" with your mortgage lender. A loan modification is when the lender agrees to temporarily lower your interest rate for a set period of time to ease your financial burden. Recent government action and your lender's motivation to have one less foreclosure make this a great option. Contact your lender directly to pursue this alternative. If they become difficult to work with, **carefully consider a loan modification company only after investigating their references and fees.**

8. If your lender refuses to cooperate, investigate filing bankruptcy. I will discuss this in depth in the next chapter.

9. Thoroughly investigate any person or company who contacts you about "rescuing" you out of foreclosure. **Multiple foreclosure "scams" are being reported from coast to coast so contact your state attorney general's office, the Better Business Bureau, or your lender before**

giving them any information or signing any documents.

Whether it's foreclosure or just falling behind on a credit card, there is no way to sugarcoat the fact that on the <u>Green Trail</u> you will have to sacrifice to find your way back to the **Bay of Great Credit**. Besides the house, you may have to sell that motorcycle you bought on impulse. When your buddies ask if you want a ticket to the big game, you'll have to say no. When your girlfriends go for a last minute casino trip, you'll have to pass.

I could literally fill an entire book with the touching stories of sacrifice of the clients I've been privileged to work with over the years. Some held three and four jobs. Others hardly had any furniture because they had sold everything to put food on the table for their children.

And why did they sacrifice?

They wanted a better life for themselves and their families. They hated the annoying phone calls from creditors more than they hated the idea of working a second job. They preferred selling their prized gun collection over the threatening letters to pay up or else. They longed to live in the **Bay of Great Credit**, and anything that made it possible was worth it.

What about you? How badly do you want it? How hard are you willing to work? How much are you willing to sacrifice?

I can only give you hope by saying you can find your way back. I can only cheer you on to the finish line. I can only tell you how to make it to the **Bay of Great Credit**.

Ultimately, though, at the end of the day, it's all about <u>**you**</u> finding your way back. No one can make you do anything. No one can do it for you. It's time for you to take a hard look in the mirror and decide what you're going to do. Which way will you go? You're on the <u>Green Trail</u>. There's a red sky in the morning.

Will you heed the warning?

Chapter 8

Yellow Trail:
Judgment Peak &
Collection Canyon

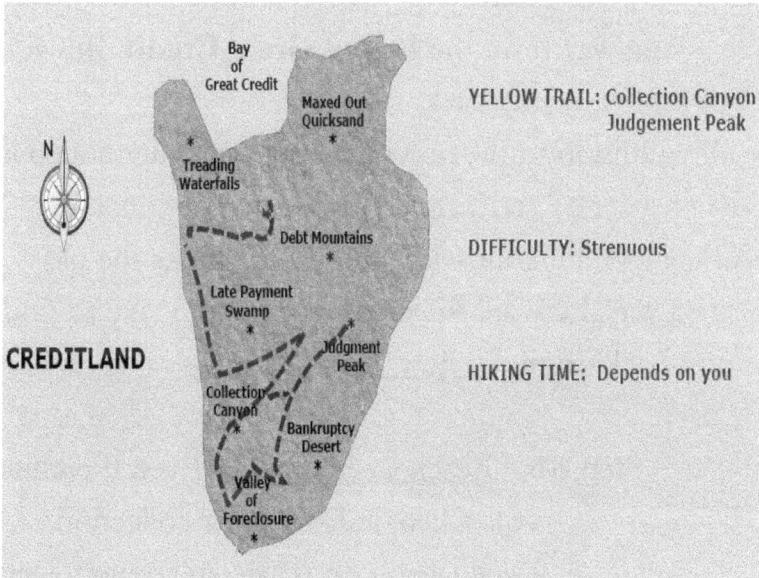

One of my friends has fourteen brothers and sisters.
I asked him once what meal times were like at his house

growing up. He replied, "Well…if you didn't get right to the table, there might not be any left!"

When it comes to the <u>Yellow Trail</u>, it's kind of like that. It's getting late in the credit game. There aren't many options left to find your way back. You're being pushed into a corner because now the **Debt Mountains** and **Late Payment Swamp** have turned into **Judgment Peak** and **Collection Canyon**. Your creditors aren't messing around. They have pursued legal action now. Some may even garnish your wages. You are staring at the biggest financial decision you've ever faced. But guess what? You're like a cat with nine lives. Sure, your credit scores are sickly, and you're a long way from the **Bay of Great Credit**. But you still can find your way back.

In addition to the previous four steps mentioned in the last chapter of verifying accurate information, consulting a credit counselor, and doing things the old fashioned way, here are the final two steps to take to find your way back on the <u>Yellow Trail</u>:

> Step #5: <u>Reach a settlement.</u> Even if creditors file a lien, judgment, or collection against you, most are still open to settle with you because they realize something is better than nothing. Right? How much a creditor will settle

for is largely determined by what type of debt the original account was. For example, credit card companies will settle for a far less percentage than the IRS. The Federal Trade Commission which governs creditors dealings with consumers released a report in October 2007 stating that the average collection creditors settled for was 16% or 16 cents for every $1 of the original debt! Keep in mind that report relates to credit card and medical collections not a short sale on your home. Your mortgage lender can't afford to take a loss like that on your home! In some cases, you may need to hire a tax attorney, credit attorney, or a consumer credit counselor, but in many cases, you can negotiate the settlement yourself!! Do *not* underestimate what **you** can do! But if no settlement can be reached, and you've done all the other steps, and your financial resources are exhausted…there's one step left…it's the bottom…it's rock bottom…

Step # 6 <u>Carefully consider bankruptcy</u>. Let me go officially on the record stating that I do not condone bankruptcy. I know from personal experience it is a nasty combination of hell and humiliation. But tell me what other options a 37 year old mother of three has when her husband dies and there is no life insurance. Or a man's employer of 31 years closes and moves to Mexico, and new jobs are scarce especially for a 55 year old. How can unemployment be enough to pay his bills?

The economy at the time of the writing of this book is approaching the depths of the Great Depression and in doing so is shattering the American dream. Add to that toxic mixture life events such as death, disability, and divorce, and it's a recipe for bankruptcy filings continuing to rise. The fact of the matter is that legitimate life occurrences corner us now and then. When they do, consult with a reliable bankruptcy attorney to see what type of bankruptcy, if any, for which you qualify. **Here are some tips for finding a good bankruptcy attorney:**

1. Verify they are a member of the state bar where you reside. Search online using the name of your state

and then add "state bar", and there should be a directory for you to search.

2. Check with your state attorney general's office for attorney referral services. Not every state has one, but if yours does, use it.

3. Check with your state's grievance commissions or discipline boards for attorneys. Avoid any attorney on the list.

4. Go to **www.avvo.com** where you can view attorney ratings.

5. Search for internet blogs about attorneys in your area. You may find a wealth of information.

6. If you know someone who filed bankruptcy or who works with bankruptcy attorneys in their industry, ask who they would recommend.

I am not a bankruptcy attorney, but I have worked with thousand of consumers who filed bankruptcy. A great resource to understand bankruptcy terminology is **www.uscourts.gov/bankruptcycourts.html**. This is THE website from the U.S. Government. There are two types of personal bankruptcy:

1. Chapter 13 Bankruptcy is where you pay back a percentage of your debts. The advantages are you and your property are protected by federal bankruptcy laws, and you may be able to keep your home and auto(s). You, your creditors, and the U.S. Bankruptcy Court reach an agreement on what accounts you pay back, as well as what percentage, and for how long up to 5 years. Once that agreement is reached a monthly payment to the trustee is set. The amount is either payroll deducted or paid directly by you to the trustee who in turn distributes it to your various creditors. Your pay history to the U.S. Bankruptcy Trustee is very important because if you miss payments, the trustee can dismiss your case and present and future lenders will dislike it. Creditors and lenders view Chapter 13 Bankruptcy more favorably because you at least paid back a percentage of your debt.

2. The second type of personal bankruptcy is Chapter 7 Bankruptcy, where you typically file for protection on all your debts. The only debts that cannot be filed in a Chapter 7 and 13 are child support, owed taxes, and student loans. In certain situations, houses and automobiles can be redeemed (kept), but consult with your attorney. Chapter 7 Bankruptcy is not viewed as favorable as a Chapter 13 by the lending

industry because you don't pay back any percentage of your debts.

Because bankruptcy has such far reaching and lasting results and consequences, I think it's important to answer the question here: **How do you know when it's time to consult a bankruptcy attorney?**

1. When you have fallen behind on your house payments to the point foreclosure proceedings have started, and you want to keep your home, contact a bankruptcy attorney. Many consumers file bankruptcy for the primary reason of rescuing their home from being foreclosed. Bankruptcy law protects and establishes a plan to catch up on what is past due.

2. When you have a foreclosure or repossession completed, consult a bankruptcy attorney. Foreclosures and repossessions typically sell below even far below what you owe, leaving you responsible for thousands, even tens of thousands, of dollars. The lender can and will come after you for that remaining balance. I know two clients right now who had foreclosures four years ago but never filed bankruptcy. Those lenders have continually pursued them for the shortage, but the clients have no means to pay

them, so they're just now finally filing bankruptcy. Remember…in the credit industry, a foreclosure is considered worse than a bankruptcy.

3. When what you owe creditors is far greater than your income, consult a bankruptcy attorney. **Perhaps divorce, illness, or job loss has buried you in debt.** Your bankruptcy attorney will compare your income to your debts using a "means test" to see if you are eligible to file bankruptcy.

This is heavy, heavy stuff. If there was ever a time you need to keep reminding yourself, "This is my *location*, <u>not</u> my *destination*", it is now. With your back against the wall, you need to believe you can recover *even* from bankruptcy.

And for those of you who think bankruptcy is the easy way out of your financial and credit crisis, I give you the <u>Red Trail</u>.

Chapter 9

The Red Trail:
Bankruptcy Desert
& Valley of Foreclosure

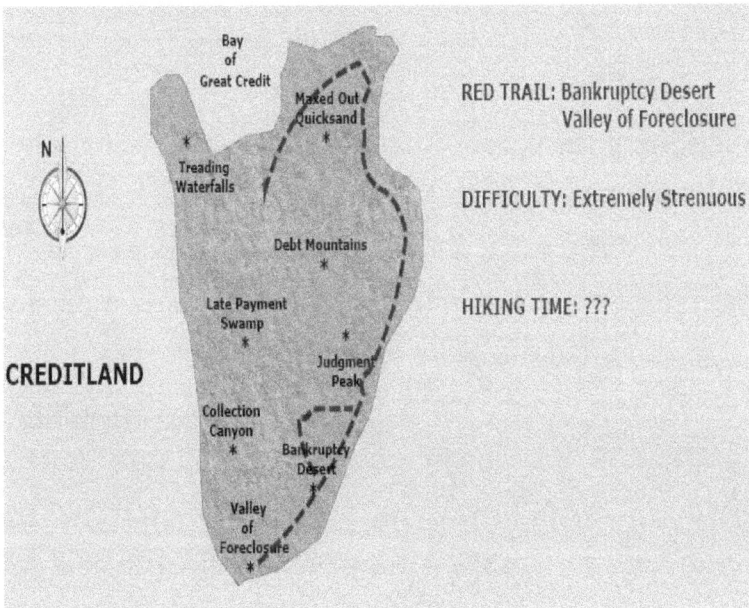

I have a stupid question: Do you enjoy root canals? If you answered "yes", then you will love the Red Trail! If you answered 'no', the only good news I can offer is that you'll love where the Red Trail takes you. Yes, the hike is hard, but it will be worth it when you dip your big toe in the **Bay of Great Credit**.

No longer will you be worrying about where you'll live. You won't be wondering if you can ever get this bankruptcy behind you. You'll be too preoccupied celebrating your escape from the wolves in the **Valley of Foreclosure** and/or **Bankruptcy Desert**. You'll be too busy celebrating because you found your way back.

Back in the 1930's, the Sierra Club devised a scale to rate the difficulty of hikes and climbs in the Sierra Nevada. If the Sierra Club rated the difficulty of the Red Trail running along the coast of Creditland, they would grade it 7, which means "Extremely Strenuous/Severe." That's why I named it the "Red" Trail; because the degree of difficulty will require so much of your attention and energy.

Part of that difficulty relates to the Red Trail's length. As you can tell by looking at the map, life after bankruptcy and foreclosure on the Red Trail is the longest trail back. You can't travel any further away from the **Bay of Great Credit** than the **Valley of Foreclosure** and **Bankruptcy Desert**.

So how long is the Red Trail you ask? That depends on what and when certain events occur.

THE STOPWATCH

The <u>Red Trail</u> stopwatch starts the second you file bankruptcy, experience foreclosure, or complete a short sale. I can think of no better analogy than a prisoner serving a mandatory sentence. When you file bankruptcy, let your property be foreclosed on, or do a short sale, some creditors have strict time guidelines (sentences so to speak) during which they will not release (lend) any money to you, regardless of your credit scores.

Like the Law telling the 14 year old, "You can't legally drive until 16", creditors will inform you, "We will not consider lending money to you until at least 24 months after your bankruptcy discharge." Your bankruptcy, foreclosure, or short sale is considered a crime by them, so they will make you do the time on the <u>Red Trail</u>, and each offense carries a different sentence. To determine how long your sentence on the <u>Red Trail</u> is, grab the paperwork I listed in Chapter 3: your bankruptcy papers, foreclosure papers (especially the Sheriff's Deed), deed in lieu of foreclosure, and short sale papers.

Here's the key information you'll need to find in these documents:

<u>If you filed bankruptcy…</u>

❖ What type of bankruptcy did you file?

- Chapter 13 Bankruptcy: You paid back a percentage of your debts by paying a weekly or monthly amount to the U.S. Bankruptcy Trustee.
- Chapter 7 Bankruptcy: You did not pay any of your debts back except for possibly reaffirming your debt on your house or car.

❖ Was your bankruptcy discharged or dismissed?
- Discharge: After following bankruptcy court requirements to completion, you have been given an order by a bankruptcy judge forgiving your debts listed in your bankruptcy papers.
- Dismissal: A bankruptcy judge has ruled your bankruptcy is dismissed before completion and your creditors can come after you for your debt.

❖ What date was your bankruptcy discharged or dismissed?

❖ <u>If you had a foreclosure, deed in lieu of foreclosure, or short sale…</u>
➢ What was the date of your foreclosure auction?
➢ What date did you sign the deed over?
➢ What date did you do the short sale?
➢ What caused your foreclosure, deed in lieu of foreclosure, or short sale?

Now that you have this vital information, complete the following checklist. Think of it this way:

Just like when you go to a new doctor, and they have you complete a "Past/Current Medical History Form", so too, you need to complete a "Past/Current Bankruptcy/Foreclosure/Short Sale History Checklist." This checklist will identify how much longer your time on the Red Trail will be. PLEASE REMEMBER TO ONLY CHECK EACH STATEMENT WHICH IS TRUE OF YOUR SITUATION:

Past/Present Bankruptcy, Foreclosure, Deed In Lieu of Foreclosure, and Short Sale Checklist

☐	1. My Chapter 13 Bankruptcy has been discharged at least one day.
☐	2. My Chapter 7 Bankruptcy has been discharged at least 24 months.
☐	3. My foreclosure auction was at least 36 months ago.
☐	4. My deed in lieu of foreclosure was at least 36 months ago.
☐	5. My short sale was at least 12 months ago.
☐	6. My Chapter 13 Bankruptcy will be discharged in 12 months or less.
☐	7. My Chapter 7 Bankruptcy was discharged at least 12 months ago.
☐	8. My foreclosure auction was at least 24 months ago.
☐	9. My deed in lieu of foreclosure was at least 24 months ago.
☐	10. My short sale was less than 12 months ago.
☐	11. My Chapter 7 Bankruptcy was discharged less than 12 months ago.
☐	12. My foreclosure auction was at least 12 months ago.
☐	13. My deed in lieu of foreclosure was at least 12 months ago.
☐	14. My foreclosure auction is scheduled or just recently completed.
☐	15. My deed in lieu of foreclosure is scheduled or was just recently completed.
☐	16. My Chapter 13 or Chapter 7 Bankruptcy was recently dismissed.
☐	17. I have had multiple bankruptcies in the last 7 years.

So here's the moment of truth for you. Some of you will dance with joy because you're about to discover you have already hiked the <u>Red Trail</u> and didn't realize it.

Others of you may curse in disappointment because you are still years away from finding your way back.

Whatever your situation is, the great news is that you can and will eventually find your way back.
Remember: THIS IS YOUR LOCATION, **NOT** YOUR DESTINATION. You are on a journey…a journey to find your way back, and right now you are on the <u>Red Trail</u>.

The <u>Red Trail</u> is intense. It flat out will test everything in you.

I know.

I've personally hiked it. I've professionally hiked it with thousands of people. Ready or not, here's the truth based on how you completed the checklist:

If you checked any statement between 1 and 5, your time left on the <u>Red Trail</u> is 0. Congratulations.
You've done your time. Oh, there's still some work to be done to completely find your way back, which I'll discuss shortly, but for now, live in the moment! You can hear the waves crashing on the beach in the **Bay of Great Credit**! You now can purchase a home through government programs such as FHA and VA (See Appendix C) at a great fixed interest rate.

Welcome back!

For the rest of you, you'll be there soon, but for now here's where you stand:

- If you checked any statement between 6 and 10, your time left on the <u>Red Trail</u> is at least one year.
- If you checked any statement between 11 and 13, you have at least two years left on the <u>Red Trail</u>.
- If you checked statement 14 or 15, you have at least three years remaining on the <u>Red Trail</u>.
- If you checked statement 16, a minimum of four years lie ahead of you on the <u>Red Trail</u>.
- If you checked statement 17, you will be on the <u>Red Trail</u> for five years or more.

Ouch. The truth hurts. I'm not saying that no one will lend money or extend credit to you during this period because some will at extremely high interest rates. What I am saying is that bankruptcy and foreclosure sentence you to a credit Antarctica. Your credit can't go any further south or farther away from the **Bay of Great Credit.**

On the <u>Red Trail</u>, there is a room I call the "Waiting Room." We enter it when we file bankruptcy, have a foreclosure, or conduct a short sale. Some of you arrived earlier than others, which is why you were able to check one or more statements between 1-5. Others of you have just arrived, and I'm glad you brought this book along to read, because it's going to be a while.

- If you filed Chapter 7 Bankruptcy, you'll be waiting two or more years after the discharge.
- If Chapter 13 Bankruptcy was filed, your time is at least one year.
- If your bankruptcy was dismissed, you'll spend four years in the waiting room.
- If you filed multiple bankruptcies in the last seven years, your wait is five years.
- With a foreclosure, you'll be waiting at least three years from the date of the sheriff's auction (sale).
- Even if you did a deed in lieu of foreclosure, the three year wait begins when you sign over the property.
- If you completed a short sale, you'll be waiting at least one year from the date of closing.

Keep in mind creditors *can* show compassion and shorten your wait if you prove what are called "extenuating circumstances." Extenuating circumstances are factors beyond your control, such as serious illness, disability, death, and employment layoff. As of the writing of this book, divorce is unfortunately NOT considered an extenuating circumstance.

Creditors review extenuating circumstances on a case by case basis, and if they agree your situation was extreme, they will reduce your waiting time by at least one year.

While you're in the waiting room…no matter if you just finished or started, the waiting room on the <u>Red Trail</u> is not for napping and marking off the days on a calendar. **It's time to take charge…control…of your dreams and life.** Here's what you need to be doing in that waiting room to find your way back:

<u>RED TRAIL "TO DO" LIST</u>

1. **Pay Attention.**

   A. Monitor <u>every</u> bill and pay it within thirty days of its due date. DO NOT LET ANYTHING GO TO COLLECTION. **When you are on the <u>Red Trail</u>, there is NO margin for error.** If creditors see a pattern of financial irresponsibility AFTER a bankruptcy, foreclosure, or short sale, they see a giant red flag and will likely refuse to lend to you. The most common mistakes I see <u>Red Trail</u> clients make are to bounce checks and/or let cell phone, medical, and utility bills go to collection. Don't do it. It's not worth it. Do whatever it takes to keep yourself on track to find your way back!

B. Regularly check your credit to make sure your creditors are accurately reporting. Again the government recommended website is **www.annualcreditreport.com**. If you discover errors, review Chapter 7 of this book regarding what to do.

C. If you had or have a bankruptcy, watch your attorneys to make sure they correctly handle your case. I say that not because I have issues with attorneys. I have worked closely with many great attorneys over the years. I have friends who are attorneys.

I, however, also know attorneys are human and can make mistakes just like you and me. **One of the best ways to help your attorney is to provide them with your complete credit report along with all the other documents they request.** I know clients who traveled the <u>Red Trail</u>, blindly trusting their lawyers to know everything about their situation and file the right paperwork. Vital paperwork was <u>not</u> filed. Critical debt was <u>not</u> included.

I have a client right now who has a post bankruptcy judgment of $39,000 because her attorney did not correctly file her paperwork. My point is to educate yourself and know the bankruptcy, foreclosure, and short sale process well enough so you can keep track of *your* bankruptcy. Between the internet, local library, and bookstores, an abundance of recent and reliable information is available so you can be an informed consumer. A little bit of work by you can pay huge dividends.

D. Be very cautious about having joint credit accounts with or cosigning for *anyone*. Do not put anyone in a position to ruin your credit! You have come too far to let that happen.

2. Start Reestablishing Good Credit.

A. Any credit card(s), auto loan(s), student loans, or mortgage(s) you still have; pay them on time. I will say it again: **When you are on the <u>Red Trail</u>, there is <u>NO</u> margin for error.** You are on thin ice as it is with creditors, and any late payments may crack the ice.

B. If you don't have any of the above, opening one or two small secured credit cards is a great way to rebuild your credit. Do your research for the best deal(s), and <u>make sure they report to the credit bureaus</u>. Guard how much you charge, because you don't want to carry a balance of more than 50% of your credit limit.

C. Sorry to sound like a broken record, but pay your utilities, cell phones, and medical bills on time and do not bounce checks! I call these "small foxes", and they are notorious for tripping those who are in the process of finding their way back.

3. Save

A. Build your savings up to at least six months of reserves. I know times are tough and money is scarce with the high cost of food, gas, and utilities. Do whatever it takes to build your "rainy day" fund, so you're not living paycheck to paycheck.

B. If owning a home is your dream, put away money for a down payment. Unless you are a qualified veteran of the United States Armed Forces or desire to live in a designated "rural" area, you will need at least a 3.5% down payment to buy a home.

C. Budgeting is a key component of saving. Learn to be a thrifty shopper. Set limits and stick to them. Take advantage of all the budgeting internet websites and computer software available.

D. Protect yourself from having "champagne taste with a beer budget." Some of you are on the <u>Red Trail</u> because your eyes were bigger than your stomach. You had to have it, but you couldn't afford it….yet you still bought it. Now, here you are. Take this time in the waiting room and use it wisely to grow as a person who lives within their means.

4. **Find a loan officer and realtor who knows and does FHA (Federal Housing Administration), VA (Veteran's Administration), and RHDA (Rural Housing Development Loans).** Just because someone works as a loan officer at a bank, credit union, or mortgage broker does not mean they know these programs. The same can be said of realtors. These loan programs give you the best bang for your buck when it comes to purchasing or refinancing a home. They provide great rates and terms, and everything about them protects the consumer! Additional information about them can be found at **www.findingyourwayback.com**.

If you will practice these four activities while in the "waiting room" on the <u>Red Trail</u>, you will resurface in the

Bay of Great Credit. In other words, **you** will find your way back.

Over the years, it has been my privilege to be the guide for thousands who have successfully found their way back on the <u>Red Trail</u>. THE number one reaction…winning by a landslide… I've heard from clients when they realize they made it is, "I can't believe it! I never thought it would happen for me!"

Perhaps you're reading this book wondering if it will happen for you.

Right now, you feel trapped; even overwhelmed. You're sick of **Bankruptcy Desert** and/or the **Valley of Foreclosure**. The heat is stifling. You wish it would rain. You wish you had a remote control with a fast forward button to jump to the end of the trail.

Although I don't know what it's like to be you, I do know what it's like to feel what you're feeling.

I know what it's like to crawl through the **Valley of Foreclosure** and **Bankruptcy Desert**.

I know what it's like to sit for years in the "waiting room", waiting for my day to come. My day came, and I can assure you one day *your* day *will* come. Yes it will.

While you're waiting, here's your assignment:

<u>Assignment</u>

1. Pick one thing you are going to do or improve on from the "To Do" list while you're waiting.
2. Repeat after me: This is my **_location_**, <u>not</u> my **_destination_**.
3. Reflect on what you're going to do when this is all over.

Chapter 10

Cool Down

Ask any personal trainer or fitness guru and they will tell you how important it is to finish an exercise routine with a cooling down period. It's a period where you slow down your activity so your heart and breathing rates return to normal which improves the overall health of your body and muscles.

Cooling down not only makes sense for physical exercise. It also sounds like wise advice for finding your way back. You've pushed and pushed to return to the **Bay of Great Credit**. You've hiked the **Debt Mountains** and weathered the **Valley of Foreclosure**. Your feet have blisters. Your brain is fried. Now what should you do? Cool down.

Here are some suggestions as you transition:

1. <u>Recognize</u> the toll finding your way back has had on you. Based on the thousands of successful returns I've witnessed, it does not matter what sex or strength you are. This journey that you just completed has drained you beyond your wildest nightmares. The stress you have survived can destroy your physical and emotional health and your relationships. Too much is at stake here for you to live in denial. This is a time for honesty and transparency. It's more than okay to admit you're exhausted.

2. In light of the above, <u>rest</u>. My grandmother said, "You can't live every second like you're killing snakes." It was her way of saying, "Chill!" Go fishing. Lay out at the pool. See a movie. Do anything which makes your mind and body forget about the war you just survived.

3. <u>Watch out</u> for predators. Like buzzards circling a carcass in the desert, there will be individuals and businesses who will think you are easy prey because of your less than perfect credit. I realize you need to establish new credit, but don't do it at the cost of 20% interest on a car loan. Loans like that can quickly throw you back on the <u>Green Trail</u>. Shop

around using the internet, and you'll discover there are national companies offering fairly competitive rates even for consumers recently out of bankruptcy.

4. <u>Live</u> like you have good credit.

   ➤ There's no need to tell others about your credit struggles unless a financial transaction is involved. It's none of their business.

   ➤ Take off the sticker or license frame on your car advertising the "buy here…pay here" auto dealer. I call those, "I have bad credit," bumper stickers.

   ➤ If you haven't yet, register for the "Do Not Call" list at **www.donotcall.gov**. You don't need to be harassed by telemarketers!

   ➤ Shred your junk mail. Marketers will bombard you with all kinds of crazy offers, and you don't need their junk.

All these small steps help you move forward with your life.

5. I've saved the best for last: <u>Party</u>. I'm not suggesting go hog wild. I simply am saying to celebrate your

return. Enjoy the moment. Toot your own horn for finding your way back. You should be very proud of yourself. Pick one thing you love and gave up to get here and do it! Attend a baseball game. Go out for a nice dinner. Enjoy a concert. You've earned it!

This may sound strange to you, but I say this out of my experience with so many who have found their way back. What you do *after* you return to the **Bay of Great Credit** is just as important as what you did to get there. I have seen too many make it back, but then they don't take the time to cool down which leads to trouble. Learn from them and take the time to cool down. You won't regret it.

Chapter 11

Maiden Voyage

April 15, 1912 the *RMS Titanic* sank on her maiden voyage. History is littered with many other examples of maiden voyage disasters, and I don't want your name to be added to the list. Reentering the water in the **Bay of Great Credit** can be hazardous. You've been stuck at the red light on Creditland for so long, and now that light has turned green. You are ready to put the petal to the metal and go from 0 to 60 in one second. And if you're not careful, you'll lose control and crash. I've watched plenty of consumers do it.

As you take your maiden voyage back into the sea of credit after finding your way back, here are some tips so *you* don't shipwreck. Keep in mind that these do not happen overnight.

1. **Put <u>your</u> wellbeing first.** Guess what? All those voices and choices screaming for you to buy and buy now do not care about *your* wellbeing. They want to use you for *their* wellbeing. If you don't put *your* wellbeing first, who will? Be good to yourself first. Living paycheck to paycheck, draining your savings, and racking up debt are not good for YOU. Eventually they will wreck your life. On the other hand, saving money and living on a budget put *your* wellbeing first.

2. **<u>Set goals</u> which put your wellbeing first. Make goals regarding...**

    A. Income potential and stability.

    ➢ Compare your income to your needs and wants. If your bills consume more than 50% of your gross (pretax) pay, you need to stick to a very strict budget.

    ➢ Perhaps you need to establish the goal of finding a new job, going back to school, or changing careers so your income can support your dreams. By the way, government student loans are not based on credit so past credit issues will not prevent you from being

approved unless you have previously
defaulted on student loans.

B. Savings and retirement.

  ➢ Calculate how much savings you need to have
    six months reserves to cover the unexpected.
    This way when your car needs new brakes or
    your son needs new glasses, you don't have to
    use credit cards. You're giving yourself a
    cushion for when life falls apart.

  ➢ List your wants such as a house or car and
    determine what down payments and prices fit
    in your budget. Many websites have loan
    calculators where you can plug in different
    amounts and see what monthly payments will
    be. Remember that to be approved for a
    mortgage your total debt to income ratio
    needs to be less than 41%.

  ➢ Reflect on at what age you want to retire. Talk
    with a financial planner and make a plan.

C. Pick a credit score you want to have.

  ➢ The long term goal is 740 and above.

  ➢ The short term goal is 620 and above. At the
    present time, most lenders and loan programs

have established 620 as the minimum credit score for loan approval.

3. <u>Take action</u> to make your goals reality.

   A. Let your budget rule your life when it comes to your income for savings, retirement, and expenses. Your credit limits are not in charge. Just because you can qualify for a loan does not mean you take the loan. Your budget is now the control center for your income and use of credit.

   B. Pursue new employment or finish your degree. Investigate online job and college websites. The possibilities are endless! Sure times are tough, but there have never been more flexible opportunities for employment and education than there are today.

   C. Clean up your credit report. For some, that means faxing in your bankruptcy paperwork to the credit bureau(s). For others, it involves paying your creditors on time. The older your late payments and credit issues are and the better your new reestablished credit is, the faster your credit scores will climb past 620 and rise towards 740.

Probably these tips are not new to you. You may have heard or read about them before your credit crisis, or you already knew you needed to do them before your bankruptcy. Like anything in real life, the difficulty is in taking what's on paper and practicing it. Most of the time we know *what* we need to do, but we *fail* to do it. Then we end up in the credit emergency room.

I don't know about you, but I certainly never ever want to return to any location in Creditland. I did not enjoy my stay! If you also desire to never return to **Late Payment Swamp, Debt Mountains, or the Valley of Foreclosure**, practice these three tips. When you do, you will not return to Creditland, nor will you sink in your maiden voyage like the *RMS Titanic*. Instead you will chart a course for smooth sailing in the **Bay of Great Credit**.

Chapter 12

For You

"Hello, Mr. Storm. I was referred to you. They said maybe you could help me with my credit situation...."

About once a day, sometimes more, I receive calls like that. Some callers are on the Blue Trail. Others are on the Red. Then, there are plenty who are on the Green and Yellow Trails.

It isn't the calls that get to me. It's what I hear in their voices. I hear the frustration. I hear the weariness. I hear their pain. I hear the defeat, and I hear their wounded spirits. I hear some losing hope. I hear some throwing in the towel.

What bothered me more than what I heard was what I couldn't do.....I couldn't help everyone who called. I couldn't help them if their credit scores were too low. I couldn't help them if they had late payments after filing bankruptcy. I couldn't help them if their home was foreclosed on last year, and I couldn't believe some of the credit and financial advice these people had been given by attorneys, banks, and loan officers.

I thought to myself, ***"If only I had been able to reach these people earlier and lay out an action plan, I would have been able to help them."***

I certainly don't know everything, but I did know what these clients needed to do.

Then I wondered if there was some book or website to refer them to for help.

Nope.

Oh, there were and are plenty of books and websites on credit, but I could find nothing like what I thought my callers and clients needed. They needed to know that this was their **location**, not their **destination**.

They needed to know the game was not over for them.

They needed to know they **could** find their way back.

They needed to know **how** to find their way back.

So I started thinking about writing a book. I bounced the idea off my clients, and the vote was unanimous: Write the book! So I did.

But I didn't write the book for me. Yes, I wrote the book out of having both personal and professional experience living and working in the trenches, but I did not write the book for me.

I wrote it for you. I saw your faces. I heard your voices. I wrote it to give you hope. I wrote it to give you a plan of action regardless of what trail you are hiking. I wrote it to cheer you on in these hard economic times. I wrote it so you could be your own "economic stimulus package". I wrote it so you could find your way back. I wrote it so you would know *how* to find your way back.

I wrote it for you.

Chapter 13

Finding Your Way Back

I don't know when, and I don't know where. I don't know exactly how, either, but you **_will_** find your way back. If *I* can, so can you.

I found my way back February 17, 2006. I found my way back in Rockford, Michigan. I found my way back when I closed on **MY** house.

Did you catch that? "**MY**" house!!! I didn't close on a "client's" house like I had done over a thousand times. I closed on **MY** house!! Want to know what I did after the closing?

I drove to **MY** house. I walked inside and ran around pumping my fists, shouting, "This is **MY** house!!!!"

If you had watched, you would have concluded either I had just won a national championship or I had lost my mind. Eventually, I settled for a floor seat in the living room, and as I looked around and the reality hit me, I was overwhelmed with emotion.

I'm not ashamed to tell you I sobbed. I sobbed as I remembered the five years of hell I had went through to sit here. I thought of the sleepless nights filled with worry and fear. I thought of the wolves of bankruptcy and foreclosure. I thought of the shame I carried inside me.

I thought of the moments when I almost lost hope that this day would ever come.

I thought of the mistakes I had made.

I thought of all the hard lessons this period in my life had taught me.

I thought of how hard I had worked to make this moment a reality.

I thought of how this house I was sitting in would for me forever symbolize finding my way back.

As I relive that life changing moment, I am sitting at my desk in that very house writing a book about helping others finding their way back; and you know what I'm thinking about right now?

I'm thinking about you. I'm visualizing that day…that moment when you too find your way back. I wonder what day of the week it will be. I wonder what month of the year. I wonder in what state and city you'll be.

I wonder how it will happen for you. I wonder if you too will run around pumping your fist in the air shouting for joy. I wonder if you will cry.

I wonder what you will think about. I wonder what physical object will forever be a symbol of you finding your way back.

The only thing I'm not wondering about as I write this is whether or not you'll find your way back. I already know you will find your way back, just as I did.

When you do, e-mail or write me your "finding my way back" story, because I love to hear them! For now, though, it's time to get moving, because this is not the ending.

This is just your beginning.

Now, go find your way back.

ADDENDIX A

Resources for Credit Reports and Consumer Rights

www.findingyourwayback.com This website contains current news, information, answers, resources, and links related to building and rebuilding your credit and how to resolve pretty much any credit situation.

www.annualcreditreport.com (877) 322-8228 This is the central website established by the three credit bureaus where they provide you access to your free annual credit report. Besides obtaining your credit report and credit scores, this is the best place to dispute any errors showing on your credit report.

www.experian.com (888) 397-3742 Experian is one of the three recognized credit bureaus to which your creditors report.

www.transunion.com (800) 916-8800 TransUnion is one of the three recognized credit bureaus to which your creditors report.

www.equifax.com (800) 685-1111 Equifax is one of the

three recognized credit bureaus to which your creditors report.

www.ftc.gov The Federal Trade Commission website is the "consumer's bible" for any and everything related to credit, creditors, and disputing mistakes on your credit report.

www.nfcc.org (800) 388-2227 *National Foundation for Credit Counseling:* When looking for a consumer credit counselor, look for one who is a member of this organization.

www.aiccca.org (866) 703-8787 *Association of Independent Consumer Credit Counseling Agencies:* When looking for a consumer credit counselor, look for one who is a member of this organization.

APPENDIX B

Resources for Attorneys, Bankruptcy, and Foreclosure

www.uscourts.gov/bankruptcycourts.html. This is THE website from the U.S. Bankruptcy Court where the entire bankruptcy process is explained including the definitions and differences of each "chapter."

www.avvo.com You can view attorney ratings here.

www.nacba.com *National Association of Consumer Bankruptcy Attorneys.* This is a national organization for consumer bankruptcy attorneys.

Hope for Homeowners program through Federal Housing Administration (FHA) call (800) 225-5342 for more information.

www.hud.gov/foreclosure/index.cfm This is a great resource where you can find information on foreclosure from the U.S. Housing and Urban Development agency.

APPENDIX C

Loan Programs

www.fha.gov Federal Housing Administration (FHA) mortgage loans are great for any credit situation. The website contains a wealth of information so you can be an informed buyer.

www.va.gov Veteran's Administration mortgage loans are the best loans available, but you have to be a qualified veteran of the Armed Forces. If you are one, this website is a must!

www.rurdev.usda.gov Not far behind FHA and VA mortgage loans in quality are Rural Housing loans. The only reason they are behind FHA is their credit criteria has higher standards, and they are restricted by geography and income.

APPENDIX D
Attorney General Contact Information By State

State	Attorney General	Phone
Alabama:	Troy King (R) 500 Dexter Avenue, Montgomery, AL 36130 http://www.ago.state.al.us	(334) 242-7300
Alaska:	Rick Svobodny (Acting) (R) P.O. Box 110300, Diamond Courthouse, Juneau, AK 99811-0300 http://www.law.state.ak.us/	(907) 465-3600
American Samoa:	Fepulea'i A. "Afa" Ripley, Jr. American Samoa Gov't, Exec. Ofc. Bldg, Utulei, Territory of American Samoa, Pago Pago, AS 96799 http://www.samoanet.com/asg/asgdla97.html	(684) 633-4163
Arizona:	Terry Goddard (D) 1275 W. Washington St., Phoenix, AZ 85007 http://www.azag.gov/	(602) 542-4266
Arkansas:	Dustin McDaniel (D) 200 Tower Bldg., 323 Center St., Little Rock, AR 72201-2610 http://www.ag.arkansas.gov/	(800) 482-8982
California:	Edmund G. "Jerry" Brown, Jr. (D) 1300 I St., Ste. 1740, Sacramento, CA 95814 http://ag.ca.gov	(916) 445-9555
Colorado:	John Suthers (R) 1525 Sherman Street, Denver, CO 80203 http://www.ago.state.co.us/index.cfm	(303) 866-4500

Connecticut: Richard Blumenthal (D)   (860) 808-5318
55 Elm St., Hartford, CT 06141-0120
http://www.ct.gov/ag/

Delaware: Joseph R. "Beau" Biden, III (D)   (302) 577-8338
Carvel State Office Bldg., 820 N. French St., Wilmington, DE 19801
http://attorneygeneral.delaware.gov/

District of Columbia: Peter Nickles (D)   (202) 727-3400
John A. Wilson Building, 1350 PA Ave, NW Suite 409, Washington, DC 20009
http://occ.dc.gov

Florida: Bill McCollum (R)   (850) 414-3300
The Capitol, PL 01, Tallahassee, FL 32399-1050
http://myfloridalegal.com/

Georgia: Thurbert E. Baker (D)   (404) 656-3300
40 Capitol Square, SW, Atlanta, GA 30334-1300
http://ganet.org/ago/

Guam: Alicia G. Limtiaco   (671) 475-3409
Judicial Center Bldg., Ste. 2-200E, 120 W. O'Brien Dr., Hagatna, Guam 96910
http://www.guamattorneygeneral.com/

Hawaii: Mark J. Bennett (R)   (808) 586-1500
425 Queen St., Honolulu, HI 96813
http://www.hawaii.gov/ag/

Idaho: Lawrence Wasden (R)   (208) 334-2400
Statehouse, Boise, ID 83720-1000
http://www2.state.id.us/ag/

Illinois: Lisa Madigan (D)   (312) 814-3000
James R. Thompson Ctr., 100 W. Randolph St., Chicago, IL 60601
http://illinoisattorneygeneral.gov/

Indiana: Greg Zoeller (R)   (317) 232-6201
Indiana Government Center South - 5th Floor, 402 West Washington Street,
Indianapolis, IN 46204
http://www.in.gov/attorneygeneral/

Iowa: Tom Miller (D)   (515) 281-5164
Hoover State Office Bldg., 1305 E. Walnut, Des Moines, IA 50319
http://www.IowaAttorneyGeneral.org

Kansas: Steve Six (D)   (785) 296-2215
120 S.W. 10th Ave., 2nd Fl., Topeka, KS 66612-1597
http://www.ksag.org/home/

Kentucky: Jack Conway (D)   (502) 696-5300
700 Capitol Avenue, Capitol Building, Suite 118, Frankfort, KY 40601
http://ag.ky.gov/

Louisiana: James D. "Buddy" Caldwell (D)   225-326-6000
P.O. Box 94095, Baton Rouge, LA 70804-4095
http://www.ag.state.la.us/

Maine: Janet T. Mills (D)   (207) 626-8800
State House Station 6, Augusta, ME 04333
http://www.state.me.us/ag

Maryland: Douglas F. Gansler (D)   (410) 576-6300
200 St. Paul Place, Baltimore, MD 21202-2202
http://www.oag.state.md.us

Massachusetts: Martha Coakley (D) (617) 727-2200
1 Ashburton Place, Boston, MA 02108-1698
http://www.mass.gov/ago/

Michigan: Mike Cox (R) (517) 373-1110
P.O. Box 30212, 525 W. Ottawa St., Lansing, MI 48909-0212
http://www.michigan.gov/ag

Minnesota: Lori Swanson (D) (651) 296-3353
State Capitol, Ste. 102, St. Paul, MN 55155
http://www.ag.state.mn.us

Mississippi: Jim Hood (D) (601) 359-3680
Department of Justice, P.O. Box 220, Jackson, MS 37205-0220
http://www.ago.state.ms.us/

Missouri: Chris Koster (D) (573) 751-3321
Supreme Ct. Bldg., 207 W. High St., Jefferson City, MO 65101
http://ago.mo.gov/

Montana: Steve Bullock (D) (406) 444-2026
Justice Bldg., 215 N. Sanders, Helena, MT 59620-1401
http://www.doj.mt.gov

Nebraska: Jon Bruning (R) (402) 471-2682
State Capitol, P.O. Box 98920, Lincoln, NE 68509-8920
http://www.ago.state.ne.us/

Nevada: Catherine Cortez Masto (D) (775) 684-1100
Old Supreme Ct. Bldg., 100 N. Carson St., Carson City, NV 89701
http://ag.state.nv.us/

New Hampshire: Kelly Ayotte (R) (603) 271-3658
State House Annex, 33 Capitol St., Concord, NH 03301-6397
http://www.state.nh.us/nhdoj/

New Jersey : Anne Milgram (D) (609) 292-8740
Richard J. Hughes Justice Complex, 25 Market St., CN 080, Trenton, NJ 08625
http://www.state.nj.us/lps/

New Mexico: Gary King (D) (505) 827-6000
P.O. Drawer 1508, Sante Fe, NM 87504-1508
http://www.nmag.gov/

New York: Andrew Cuomo (D) (518) 474-7330
Dept. of Law - The Capitol, 2nd fl., Albany, NY 12224
http://www.oag.state.ny.us

North Carolina: Roy Cooper (D) (919) 716-6400
Dept. of Justice, P.O. Box 629, Raleigh, NC 27602-0629
http://www.ncdoj.gov/

North Dakota: Wayne Stenehjem (R) (701) 328-2210
State Capitol, 600 E. Boulevard Ave., Bismarck, ND 58505-0040
http://www.ag.state.nd.us

Northern Mariana Islands: Gregory Baka (Acting) (670) 664-2333
Office of the Attorney General N. Mariana Islands, Administration Building, Saipan,
MP 96950
http://www.cnmiago.gov/mp/

Ohio: Richard Cordray (D) (614) 466-4320
State Office Tower, 30 E. Broad St., Columbus, OH 43266-0410

http://www.ag.state.oh.us

Oklahoma: W. A. Drew Edmondson (D)   (405) 521-3921
State Capitol, Rm. 112, 2300 N. Lincoln Blvd., Oklahoma City, OK 73105
http://www.oag.state.ok.us

Oregon: John Kroger (D)   (503) 378-4732
Justice Bldg., 1162 Court St., NE, Salem, OR 97301
http://www.doj.state.or.us

Pennsylvania: Tom Corbett (R)   (717) 787-3391
1600 Strawberry Square, Harrisburg, PA 17120
http://www.attorneygeneral.gov

Puerto Rico: Antonio Sagardia   (787) 721-2900
GPO Box 902192, San Juan, PR 00902-0192
http://www.justicia.gobierno.pr

Rhode Island: Patrick C. Lynch (D)   (401) 274-4400
150 S. Main St., Providence, RI 02903
http://www.riag.state.ri.us

South Carolina: Henry McMaster (R)   (803) 734-3970
Rembert C. Dennis Office Bldg., P.O. Box 11549, Columbia, SC 29211-1549
http://www.scattorneygeneral.org

South Dakota: Larry Long (R)   (605) 773-3215
1302 East Highway 14, Suite 1, Pierre, SD 57501-8501
http://www.state.sd.us/attorney/

Tennessee: Robert E. Cooper, Jr. (D)   (615) 741-5860
500 Charlotte Ave., Nashville, TN 37243

Texas: Greg Abbott (R)   (512) 463-2100
Capitol Station, P.O. Box 12548, Austin, TX 78711-2548
http://www.oag.state.tx.us

Utah: Mark Shurtleff (R)   (801) 538-9600
State Capitol, Rm. 236, Salt Lake City, UT 84114-0810
http://attorneygeneral.utah.gov/

Vermont: William H. Sorrell (D)   (802) 828-3173
109 State St., Montpelier, VT 05609-1001
http://www.atg.state.vt.us/

Virgin Islands: Vincent Frazer   (340) 774-5666
Dept. of Justice, G.E.R.S. Complex 488-50C Kronprinsdens Gade, St. Thomas, VI 00802

Virginia: Bill Mlms (R)   (804) 786-2071
900 East Main Street Richmond, VA 23219
http://www.oag.state.va.us/

Washington: Rob McKenna (R)   (360) 753-6200
1125 Washington St. SE, PO Box 40100, Olympia, WA 98504-0100
http://www.atg.wa.gov/

West Virginia: Darrell V. McGraw, Jr. (D)   (304) 558-2021
State Capitol, 1900 Kanawha Blvd. , E., Charleston, WV 25305
http://www.wvago.us/

Wisconsin: J.B. Van Hollen (R)   (608) 266-1221
State Capitol, Ste. 114 E., P.O. Box 7857, Madison, WI 53707-7857

http://www.doj.state.wi.us

On the following page, there is a message I invite you to remove from this book. It's a message I encourage you to put on your refrigerator, mirror, desk, or some other place where you will regularly see it. It's a message I hope you read out loud and memorize.

THIS IS MY LOCATION, NOT MY DESTINATION!™